## TABLE OF CONTENTS



*Novel-Ties® are printed on recycled paper.*

## For the Teacher

This reproducible study guide consists of lessons to use in conjunction with the book *Mrs. Frisby and the Rats of NIMH.* Written in chapter-by-chapter format, the guide contains a synopsis, pre-reading activities, vocabulary and comprehension exercises, as well as extension activities to be used as follow-up to the novel.

In a homogeneous classroom, whole class instruction with one title is appropriate. In a heterogeneous classroom, reading groups should be formed: each group works on a different novel at its reading level. Depending upon the length of time devoted to reading in the classroom, each novel, with its guide and accompanying lessons, may be completed in three to six weeks.

Begin using NOVEL-TIES for reading development by distributing the novel and a folder to each child. Distribute duplicated pages of the study guide for students to place in their folders. After examining the cover and glancing through the book, students can participate in several pre-reading activities. Vocabulary questions should be considered prior to reading a chapter; all other work should be done after the chapter has been read. Comprehension questions can be answered orally or in writing. The classroom teacher should determine the amount of work to be assigned, always keeping in mind that readers must be nurtured and that the ultimate goal is encouraging students' love of reading.

The benefits of using NOVEL-TIES are numerous. Students read good literature in the original, rather than in abridged or edited form. The good reading habits, formed by practice in focusing on interpretive comprehension and literary techniques, will be transferred to the books students read independently. Passive readers become active, avid readers.

## SYNOPSIS

Mrs. Frisby, a field mouse, is the widowed mother of four young mice. The family lives comfortably on Mr. Fitzgibbon's farm until Timothy, the youngest and frailest of her offspring develops pneumonia.

Mrs. Frisby goes to her late husband Jonathan's friend, the old white mouse Mr. Ages, to get Timothy some medicine. On the way home she frees Jeremy, a crow who is caught in some string. Timothy responds to the medicine, but Mr. Ages warns that the ailing mouse must not be moved for three weeks. Moving Day, however, the day when the mouse family must move to their summer home because of spring plowing, is only five days away. Mrs. Frisby takes Jeremy's advice and goes to ask the owl what she should do. He suggests that she move her home to a safer place, seeking help with the move from a group of special rats living under the rosebush on the farm.

The rats tell her about their own past, and how her husband and Mr. Ages had escaped with them from the National Institute for Mental Health (a.k.a. NIMH) where scientists had given them injections to increase their intelligence and life-span. After their daring escape from NIMH, the rodents spent the winter in a deserted mansion reading, practicing writing, and thinking about the healthy, thriving society they planned to create. When they left the mansion, they found the abandoned, well-stocked wagon of a toy repairman from which they took tools and small motors to begin developing their own community. The leaders, afraid that their lives were becoming too easy and feeling that their society was dependent on thievery, planned to leave the farm and set up a new homeland in Thorn Valley.

After telling Mrs. Frisby their story, the rats agree to move her house to the spot selected by the owl. Meanwhile, several dissident rats have left the colony and were accidentally electrocuted stealing motors from a hardware store, alerting the psychologists of NIMH. Mrs. Frisby, captured in the farmhouse kitchen by Billy Fitzgibbon while pouring sleeping powder into Dragon the cat's bowl, overhears news about a government plan to recapture the rats. One of the rats frees Mrs. Frisby. When she warns him of the government plan, the rats decide to move to Thorn Valley immediately. After they move Mrs. Frisby's house out of the plow's path, most of the rats leave, arriving safely in Thorn Valley.

Mrs. Frisby's family is safe on the farm. Once Timothy is fully recovered, they move to their summer home where Mrs. Frisby tells her children the whole incredible story.

## PRE-READING ACTIVITIES

1. Preview the book by reading the title and the author's name and by looking at the illustration on the cover. What do you think the book will be about? Do you think it will be a realistic novel or a fantasy? Have you read any other books by Robert O'Brien?

2. For many years scientists have been using animals in experiments. Discuss the kinds of experiments you know about. What kinds of animals have been used? Why were these animals chosen? What are the results of these experiments?

3. The National Institute for Mental Health, which is referred to in this book, actually exists. Do some research to learn where it is located; the areas of its concern; its accomplishments; and the role it might play at the time of a national health emergency. If possible, locate newspaper or magazine articles that refer to this agency and display them on the class bulletin board as you read the book.

4. **Science Connection:** The science of genetics refers to the study of genes, the basic units of heredity. As knowledge about genes increases, more and more scientists are becoming involved in the field of genetic engineering. Scientists hope that manipulation of genetic material will result in new cures for disease, eradication of hereditary diseases, and an overall improvement in the human condition. Can you imagine any serious problems that might be caused by genetic engineering? What are some of the results of genetic engineering that you know about today? Do you think it should be permitted, allowed under government regulation, or banned altogether? Do some research on cloning to find out what has been accomplished in the cloning of animals. How have the accomplishments in this field been applied to humans?

5. What are some of the problems families face when they move to another community? Have you ever moved to another house in your community or out of your community? What problems did you and other members of your family face? How did you deal with these problems?

6. Describe some books where animals behave much as though they were human. What techniques might an author use to make you believe the animals are like humans? Why might an author tell a story using animals as if they were people?

7. Consider some books or films that are fantasies. What imaginary elements are contrary to reality? What parts of these books are fantastic? What parts are realistic? Do any of these books contain an important message about life?

8. Do you think it is ever all right to steal? If so, under what conditions might you condone stealing? Why do governments make stealing illegal?

## THE SICKNESS OF TIMOTHY FRISBY; MR. AGES; THE CROW AND THE CAT

**Vocabulary:** Draw a line from each word on the left to its definition on the right. Then use the numbered words to fill in the blanks in the sentences below.

| | | | |
|---|---|---|---|
| 1. | rancid | a. | with certainty |
| 2. | authoritatively | b. | without stopping |
| 3. | warily | c. | lasting for a time only; not permanent |
| 4. | relentlessly | d. | left completely; deserted |
| 5. | hypochondriac | e. | person who imagines sickness |
| 6. | abandoned | f. | affected with mental disorder, usually due to fever |
| 7. | temporary | g. | spoiled and smelling bad |
| 8. | delirious | h. | carefully |

. . . . . . . . . . . . . . . . . . . . . . . . . . . . . . . . . . . . . . . . . . . . . . . .

1. You may become ill if the food you eat is ___________________.
2. If you seem to be sick very often, people may think you are a(n) ___________________.
3. As we rushed to catch the plane, the clock ticked ___________________.
4. The doctor suggested we cool my sister's feverish body before she became ___________________.
5. Although she was younger than the other students, she spoke ___________________ about aviation, the subject she knew best.
6. Knowing they would remain for only a night, the campers put up a(n) ___________________ shelter.
7. Because of the constant threat of cats, the birds ___________________ their nest in the elm near our house.
8. If you go skating on a newly frozen pond, you must proceed ___________________.

Read to find out how Mrs. Frisby reveals her courage.

**Questions:**

1. Why did the Frisby family feel lucky in the place that they lived?
2. Why did Mrs. Frisby need to look for food in winter?
3. What surprised Mrs. Frisby on her food-hunting walk?

## The Sickness of Timothy Frisby; Mr. Ages; The Crow and the Cat (cont.)

4. Why did Mrs. Frisby seek the help of Mr. Ages?
5. Why was it courageous of Mrs. Frisby to help Jeremy?

### Questions for Discussion:

1. Do you think Jeremy will fulfill his promise to Mrs. Frisby?
2. What kinds of dangers do mice typically face?

### Literary Device: Anthropomorphism

Anthropomorphism is a literary device in which an author grants human qualities to animals. How does the author make the reader feel that Mrs. Frisby is like a human being? What are Mrs. Frisby's human qualities? How is she like a human mother?

### Literary Element: Characterization

Fill in the chart below with information you learned about Mrs. Frisby and her family. Add to the chart as you continue to read the book.

| | Physical Traits | Personality Traits |
|---|---|---|
| Mrs. Frisby | | |
| Teresa | | |
| Martin | | |
| Cynthia | | |
| Timothy | | |

## The Sickness of Timothy Frisby; Mr. Ages; The Crow and the Cat (cont.)

### Science Connection:

Use an encyclopedia, a medical reference book, or the internet to learn about the disease pneumonia. What is the disease? How is it treated? How serious is the disease today? How did the development of antibiotics affect the treatment of pneumonia?

### Writing Activity:

Mrs. Frisby, despite grave dangers, rescued the crow. Write about a time when you did a great favor for someone else or a great favor was done for you. Tell if that favor was ever repaid.

## MR. FITZGIBBON'S PLOW; FIVE DAYS; A FAVOR FROM JEREMY; THE OWL

**Vocabulary:** Use the context to figure out the meaning of the underlined word in each of the following sentences. Then draw a line from each word on the left to its definition on the right.

- From her vantage point on the hill, she could see the entire valley below.
- After hiking through the woods all day, we came upon a gloomy and primeval spot.
- After a long, slow climb up the hill, we were delighted that our descent was fast and easy.
- We were astonished to see a hawk plummet from the sky to catch a small rodent in its beak.
- After running for two hours, a five-minute rest was too short a respite.
- As dusk approached, we found it difficult to follow the trail.
- We missed the entrance to the rat hole because it was concealed by tangles of fiercely sharp thorns.
- The protesting crowd around the building was so dense that I was unable to enter.

. . . . . . . . . . . . . . . . . . . . . . . . . . . . . . . . . . . . . . . . . . . . . . . . .

| | |
|---|---|
| 1. vantage | a. hidden |
| 2. primeval | b. fall straight down |
| 3. descent | c. thick |
| 4. plummet | d. period of relief; a pause |
| 5. respite | e. period of partial darkness between day and night |
| 6. dusk | f. favorable position |
| 7. concealed | g. of earliest times; primitive |
| 8. dense | h. downward movement |

Read to find out why Mrs. Frisby feared moving day.

**Questions:**

1. How did Mrs. Frisby know that Moving Day was drawing near? Why did this worry her?
2. What strange behavior did Mrs. Frisby observe in the cat? What was odd about the rats' behavior? Why do you think they behaved this way?
3. How did Jeremy repay Mrs. Frisby's favor?

## Mr. Fitzgibbon's Plow; Five Days; A Favor from Jeremy; The Owl (cont.)

4. What did Mrs. Frisby mean when she said that knowing "something about the dietary habits of owls, . . . she did not like the idea of being trapped in his house"?

### Questions for Discussion:

1. What do you think Mrs. Frisby's husband meant when he said, "All doors are hard to unlock until you have the key"? How might this relate to Mrs. Frisby's current predicament?
2. Mrs. Frisby, trying to be a very good mother, did not tell her children that Moving Day was drawing near. Do you think that was a wise decision? Do you think parents should keep important information like this from their children? What happens in your family?

### Literary Device: Simile

A simile is a figure of speech in which two objects are compared using the words "like" or "as." For example:

The rats looked as well drilled as a group of soldiers.

What is being compared?

___

Find two other similes in this chapter. Provide page numbers.

___

___

___

___

### Science Connection:

Even though this book is part fantasy, the author imparts a great deal of scientific information, mainly about the way animals live. What information have you gotten from these chapters about how mice live in winter and summer, the characteristics of a shrew, the intelligence of a crow, how birds fly, and the habits and habitat of a nocturnal creature, such as an owl?

### Writing Activity:

Write about a time when you had a problem that you could not solve alone. Where did you seek help? What advice was offered? Did you follow the advice? What were the consequences of your decision?

## "GO TO THE RATS"; IN THE ROSEBUSH; BRUTUS

**Vocabulary:** Synonyms are words with similar meanings. Draw a line from each word in column A to its synonym in column B. Then use the words in column A to fill in the blanks in the sentences below.

| A | B |
|---|---|
| 1. agitated | a. loving |
| 2. affectionate | b. puzzled |
| 3. linger | c. suspended |
| 4. deference | d. respect |
| 5. trespassers | e. disturbed |
| 6. bewildered | f. friendly |
| 7. cordial | g. intruders |
| 8. adjourned | h. delay |

. . . . . . . . . . . . . . . . . . . . . . . . . . . . . . . . . . . . . . . . . . . . . . . . .

1. The host at the party was so ________________ that everyone was eager to return for another occasion.
2. I want to ________________ indoors when the weather is cold and windy outside.
3. A sign at the entrance to the private park warned ________________ that they would be fined.
4. My grandfather was seated at the head of the table in ________________ to his age.
5. The bird became ________________ when people came close to its nest.
6. Our lengthy meeting was ________________ when everyone had to go home for dinner.
7. I prefer a(n) ________________ puppy to one that sleeps a lot and ignores me.
8. When she saw the ________________ faces staring back at her, the teacher realized that no one understood the lesson.

**Etymology: Eavesdrop**

"Eavesdrop" means to listen secretly to a private conversation. It comes from an earlier word, *eavesdrip*, derived from Old English, meaning water that drips from the eaves of a roof. It referred to a person standing under the eaves in order to overhear a private conversation inside a house.

## "Go to the Rats"; In the Rosebush; Brutus (cont.)

Read to find out why Mrs. Frisby gets to see Nicodemus.

**Questions:**

1. What was the owl's attitude toward Mrs. Frisby when she first approached him? What caused the change in his attitude?
2. How were the owl's and Mrs. Frisby's predicaments alike?
3. Why was Mrs. Frisby becoming less afraid to fly?
4. How did Timothy know that Moving Day was near? Why did Mrs. Frisby think that Timothy "had somehow switched their positions"?
5. Why was Mrs. Frisby able to get to see Nicodemus when she returned to the Rosebush with Mrs. Ages? Why did Mrs. Frisby now ask herself ""Who am I, then"?

**Questions for Discussion:**

1. Why do you think the owl suggested that Mrs. Frisby seek help from the rats?
2. The author has created an atmosphere of growing mystery and suspense by leaving many unanswered questions in the minds of the readers. What is mysterious about the rats and the place where they live? What is mysterious about the late Mr. Frisby? What other questions do you have?

**Writing Activity:**

Use your imagination to write what you think will happen when Mrs. Frisby sees Nicodemus. Tell what you think she will learn about the rats and her late husband. After you read the book, compare what you predicted with what the author actually wrote.

## IN THE LIBRARY; ISABELLA; A POWDER FOR DRAGON

**Vocabulary:** Antonyms are words with opposite meanings. Draw a line from each word in column A to its antonym in column B. Then use the words in column A to fill in the blanks in the sentences below.

| A | B |
|---|---|
| 1. recessed | a. friendly |
| 2. destination | b. deep |
| 3. hostile | c. start |
| 4. deserted | d. slowly |
| 5. drowsy | e. bulging |
| 6. shallow | f. happy |
| 7. swiftly | g. awake |
| 8. glum | h. occupied |

. . . . . . . . . . . . . . . . . . . . . . . . . . . . . . . . . . . . . . . . . . . . . . .

1. All the children became ________________ when they learned that the carnival was canceled.
2. Everyone worried that the two ________________ nations would go to war to settle their differences.
3. Since I do not swim well, I chose to enter the pool at the ________________ end.
4. We plan to make several stops at scenic places on the way to our ________________.
5. Our canoe was tossed about in the ________________ moving current of the river.
6. We placed the statue on the ________________ shelf in the living room.
7. It was amazing to see how a once-busy city could become a ________________ ghost town.
8. After a day of exercise and hard work, I became ________________ and fell asleep immediately after dinner.

> Read to find out why Mrs. Frisby puts her life at risk.

**Questions:**

1. What unusual objects did Mrs. Frisby observe in the rats' hideaway?
2. What was Justin referring to when he mentioned "the annual light bulb harvest"?
3. What did Mrs. Frisby learn from her talk with Isabella?

## In the Library; Isabella; A Powder for Dragon (cont.)

4. How could the rats help Mrs. Frisby?
5. Why was Nicodemus reluctant to allow Mrs. Frisby to put the poison in Dragon's food?

**Art Activities:**

1. Use the information the author provides to depict the rats' hideaway. You may draw a mural, make a diorama, construct the dwelling, or use any materials you choose.
2. Use the information from the chapter titled "A Powder for Dragon" and draw sketches of the new location for Mrs. Frisby's home in the lee of the stone. One sketch should show a side view, the other should show a bird's-eye view, the scene from above.

| Side View | Bird's-eye View |
| --- | --- |
| | |

**Science Connection:**

Do some research on rats and mice, the two main species of rodents referred to in this book. Compare and contrast their habits, the places they live, their food, and their levels of intelligence. Discuss why rats are more feared than mice. Is this fear justified?

**Writing Activity:**

Imagine that Mrs. Frisby, facing the dangerous mission before her, decides to write a letter to her children. In that imaginary letter, tell them what you are about to do, the reason you are putting yourself at risk, and express your feelings and hopes for the future of your children.

## THE MARKETPLACE; IN THE CAGE; THE MAZE

**Vocabulary:** Use the words in the Word Box and the clues below to complete the crossword puzzle.

*WORD BOX*

| | | |
|---|---|---|
| compiled | eager | maze |
| confident | frenzy | second |
| contrite | futile | |
| converge | interior | |

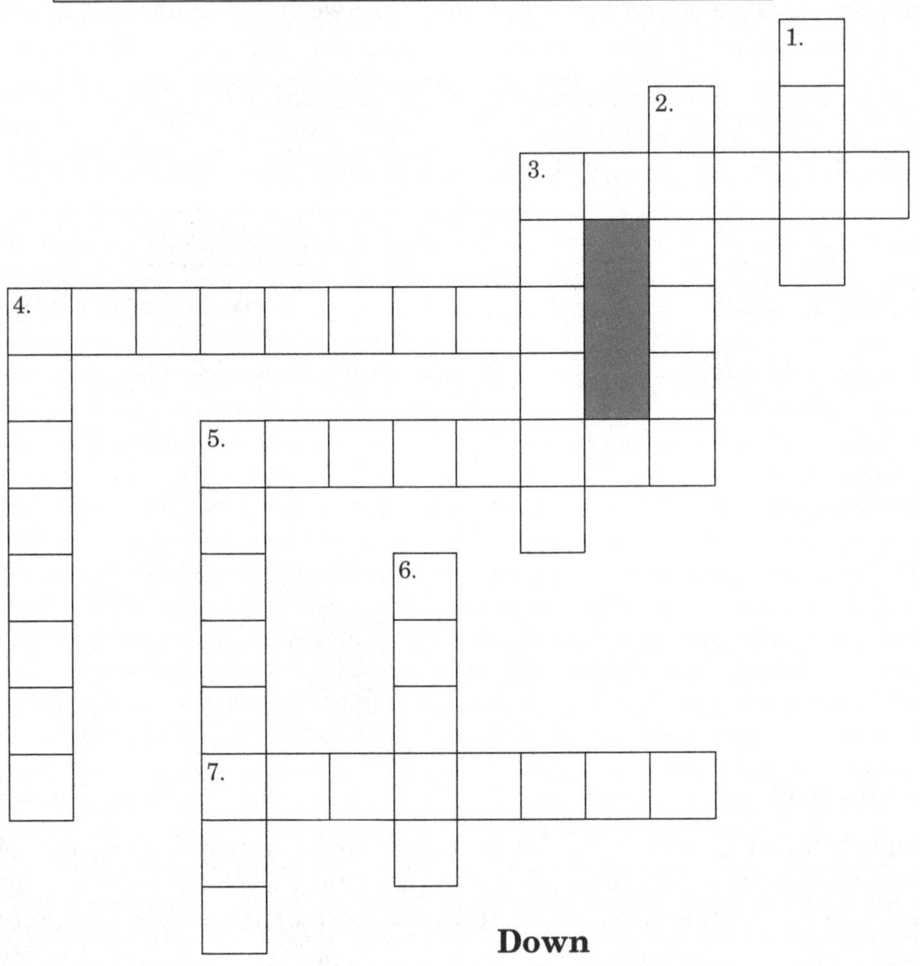


**Across**

3. wild excitement
4. certain; positive
5. put together in one book or work
7. inside

**Down**

1. complex system that causes confusion
2. next after the first
3. useless
4. come together
5. showing sincere remorse
6. impatiently wanting

## The Marketplace; In the Cage; The Maze (cont.)

**Background Information:**

Learn the meaning of these terms to better understand the following chapters:

- DNA — material that transfers genetic characteristics in all life forms
- gene — basic physical unit of heredity; a sequence of nucleotides along a segment of DNA that provides the coded instruction for an individual's hereditary character
- chromosome — any of several threadlike bodies that carry the genes in a linear order
- control group — group of subjects in an experiment who closely resemble the treatment group, but who do not receive the active medication or factor under study. They serve as a comparison group when treatment results are evaluated
- mutation — sudden departure from the parent type in one or more inherited characteristics caused by a change in a gene or a chromosome.

Read to learn about the rats' experiences at NIMH.

**Questions:**

1. How had Nicodemus come to NIMH?
2. Why were the rats captured?
3. What kinds of experiments did Nicodemus describe?
4. How did the rats feel about being at NIMH?
5. Why was Justin confident that Dr. Schultz would not harm him, even if he attempted to escape?
6. Why didn't the doctors panic when Justin escaped? What did they learn about the experimental rats during the attempted escape? What did A-9 discover while he was out of his cage?

**Literary Devices:**

I. *Flashback* — A flashback is a device in film or in literature in which an event at an earlier time is presented in order to make the current time more clear. The chapter "The Marketplace" begins a long flashback telling the story of the rats of NIMH. Now that you have read about the place where they live and have learned how they live, list some questions you would like Nicodemus to answer about his past as he talks to Mrs. Frisby.

___

___

___

## The Marketplace; In the Cage; The Maze (cont.)

II. *Cliffhanger* — A cliffhanger in literature is a device borrowed from silent, serialized film in which an episode ends at a moment of heightened tension or suspense. Its purpose is to encourage the reader to continue on to the next section. What is the cliffhanger at the end of the chapter titled "The Maze"?

______________________________________________

What do you think Justin will do?

______________________________________________

______________________________________________

______________________________________________

**Science Connections:**

1. Do some research to find out all you can about DNA, the material that transfers genetic material in all life forms. Try to find newspaper or magazine articles that deal with recent DNA research.
2. Do some research to find out about the group of compounds known as steroids. Why have they been used by some athletes? What is controversial about their use? Are there any ways in which their use has been beneficial?
3. Find books in the field of behavioral psychology that describe experiments that have been done on rats in mazes. Why do you think rats are often used for scientific experiments? Draw a diagram of a maze such as the one Nicodemus was placed into for the experiment on memory and intelligence.

**Writing Activity:**

Imagine that you are Julie and write a journal entry for the day Justin [A-9] escaped from his cage. Describe your observations, your feelings about what has occurred, and what you think the future holds for these animal experiments.

## A LESSON IN READING; THE AIR DUCTS; THE BONIFACE ESTATE

**Vocabulary:** Draw a line from each word on the left to its meaning on the right. Then use the numbered words to fill in the blanks in the sentences below.

| | | | |
|---|---|---|---|
| 1. | astute | a. | something that separates or divides |
| 2. | reluctantly | b. | unwillingly |
| 3. | consternation | c. | once in a while |
| 4. | occasionally | d. | managed skillfully |
| 5. | discontent | e. | clever |
| 6. | partition | f. | friendship |
| 7. | manipulated | g. | dissatisfaction |
| 8. | comradeship | h. | dismay; dread |

. . . . . . . . . . . . . . . . . . . . . . . . . . . . . . . . . . . . . . . . . . . . . . .

1. To our ____________________, the teacher said we would have a test.
2. It takes a(n) ____________________ mind to figure out a complicated puzzle.
3. A feeling of ____________________ developed among the campers after a week of survival training.
4. She plays tennis ____________________ even though she prefers the game of racquetball.
5. A simple ____________________ was built to turn one large bedroom into two.
6. I had a feeling of ____________________ when I faced my diet dinner and saw how little there was to eat.
7. The juggler ____________________ seven balls in the air at once.
8. The team returned to the locker room ____________________ after they lost the game.

Read to find out how the rats escaped from NIMH.

**Questions:**

1. What were the unexpected results of the experimental treatment on the rats during the training period?
2. How did the scientists teach the rats to read?
3. How did Nicodemus define reading?
4. How did the rats take advantage of their new ability to read?

## A Lesson in Reading; The Air Ducts; The Boniface Estate (cont.)

5. What problems did Jenner foresee when they were about to escape?
6. What was revealed about Jonathan Frisby on the night of the escape?
7. How did the rats escape from NIMH? How had the experiments prepared them for the escape?
8. What did the rats like best about the Boniface Estate?

**Questions for Discussion:**

Even though the precise experiments discussed in this book are fictitious, they are similar to those that are actually conducted in scientific laboratories. Do you think it is fair and just to conduct experiments on living creatures? Do you think it is all right to use rats as experimental animals?

**Writing Activity:**

While telling his story to Mrs. Frisby, Nicodemus describes how he learned to read. Search your own memory for your first experiences with independent reading. Write about how and when you first learned to read. Tell what you remember about the first books you read.

## SPECIAL ACTIVITY: A Lesson in Reading

Imagine that you have been taken prisoner by creatures from outer space who speak and write a different language from ours. You are locked in a cage on a spaceship returning to their planet. Your only hope for escape is to get out of the cage and then free your fellow prisoners. The sign on the front of your cage contains the following message.

△⋀ ⋀⊥⦸> ↃL⊐⦸ △∇⊏> ♀⋀┘⦸⊏

□L>✱♀⦸ L⊏⋀∇>✱ △┘όↃ⦸

If you can read the sign it may help you escape from the cage. See if you can figure out how to read the sign. Here are some hints.

A sign over the door says ⦸+ό△ (exit)

The faucets are labeled □⋀△ (hot) Ↄ⋀♀✱ (cold)

One elevator button says ∇⊥ (up)

The other button says ✱⋀▽> (down)

The green light says ⊐⋀ (go)

The red light says Γ△⋀⊥ (stop)

Another sign says ┘L♀⊗ ✱⋀ >⋀△ ⊏∇> (walk do not run)

Using the clues in these statements, can you figure out the sign over your cage? See if you can substitute letters for the symbols and read the sign on the front of your cage.

___

___

___

## THE MAIN HALL; THE TOY TINKER; THORN VALLEY

**Vocabulary:** Use the context to figure out the meaning of the underlined word in each of the following sentences. Then compare your definition with a dictionary definition.

1. I was so engrossed in the book I was reading that I did not see my guests arrive.
   Your definition ____________________
   Dictionary definition ____________________

2. The runner proved to those who were skeptical that he could break new records.
   Your definition ____________________
   Dictionary definition ____________________

3. Before trying to solve the difficult problem alone, you should confer with experts.
   Your definition ____________________
   Dictionary definition ____________________

4. Once we have cleared and cultivated the land, we can begin our first planting.
   Your definition ____________________
   Dictionary definition ____________________

5. As soon as I saw my parents in the audience, I intentionally sang louder.
   Your definition ____________________
   Dictionary definition ____________________

6. Being a pessimist, I am convinced that I will never reach my goal.
   Your definition ____________________
   Dictionary definition ____________________

Read to find out what advice the owl offered the rats.

**Questions:**

1. What was the Plan? How did the rats expect to carry it out?
2. What did the rats learn about their species from encyclopedias?
3. What did the rats get from the Toy Tinker? Why were these objects right for them?
4. Why did Nicodemus and the other rats become dissatisfied with life on the farm?
5. How did Nicodemus choose Thorn Valley as the site of a future home for the rats?
6. Why did Jenner say "people are our cows" to justify the rats' new life style?

## The Main Hall; The Toy Tinker; Thorn Valley (cont.)

### Questions for Discussion:

Do you think it is necessary to face difficult challenges and overcome serious obstacles in order to become a worthwhile individual? And conversely, do you think it is possible for those who have led an easy life to reach their potential?

### Science Connection:

When Nicodemus told Mrs. Frisby what he had learned about rats in the encyclopedia, he was referring to the subject of evolution, a theory that has always created controversy. Do some research on the subject and find out about Charles Darwin, the originator of the theory of natural selection.

### Art Activity:

Design a shoe box diorama, draw a diagram, paint a mural, or draw a picture of one part of the rats' habitat.

### Special Activity: Debate

Nicodemus and Jenner had opposing views about the best way for the rats to live their lives. Use a chart, such as the one below, to note the reasons for each character's opinion. Using these notes, conduct a classroom debate with one person representing Nicodemus and the other representing Jenner. Allow a set amount of time for argument and then rebuttal. The class can vote on which person presented the most effective argument.

| Nicodemus | Jenner |
|---|---|
| | |

### Writing Activity:

Write about a time when you or someone you know had to make a choice between an easy, comfortable experience and a dangerous, more challenging one. Describe the choice that was made and the consequences of that choice.

## CAPTURED; SEVEN DEAD RATS; ESCAPE

**Vocabulary:** Word analogies are equations in which the first pair of words has the same relationship as the second pair of words. For example, CAPTURED is to ESCAPED as COMMENCED is to ENDED. Both pairs of words are opposites. Choose the best word from the Word Box to complete each of the analogies below.

| *WORD BOX* | | | |
|---|---|---|---|
| baffled | enormous | schedule | vertical |
| criticized | impasse | ventilation | |

1. DEFIANT is to REBELLIOUS as ________________ is to ADMONISHED.
2. ADMIRED is to DENOUNCED as ________________ is to HORIZONTAL.
3. CORRIDOR is to PASSAGE as ________________ is to CONFUSED.
4. HUGE is to ________________ as SLY is to WILY.
5. TRAGEDY is to COMEDY as ________________ is to SOLUTION.
6. STATIONERY is to LETTER as CALENDAR is to ________________.
7. RADIATOR is to HEAT as FAN is to ________________.

Read to find out about the dangers that Mrs. Frisby and the rats face.

**Questions:**

1. Why didn't Jonathan ever tell Mrs. Frisby about NIMH?
2. Why did Jenner leave? What happened to him?
3. Why did the rats plan to destroy their cave and the machines?
4. Why did Mrs. Frisby have to put sleeping powder in Dragon's bowl?
5. What happens to Mrs. Frisby? What is the curved ceiling with little half moons that Mrs. Frisby sees before she hits a wall of metal?
6. What important news does Mrs. Frisby overhear?
7. Why does Mr. Fitzgibbon think they want to destroy the rats? Why do you think they would want to do this?
8. Why does Justin decide not to open the door of the cage but take out the rings that hold its hinges, instead?

## Captured; Seven Dead Rats; Escape (cont.)

### Science Connection:

The rats were able to move Mrs. Frisby's home using a combination of levers and pulleys. Read about these simple machines to learn how they help perform basic tasks. Draw a diagram to show how one of these machines allowed the rats to move the cinder block, or do an experiment with something in your own world to test how levers and/or pulleys will permit you to accomplish a task more easily.

### Writing Activity:

Imagine that you are Billy and you have just discovered the mouse's escape from the cage. Write a journal entry in which you describe how you caught the mouse, how you think it got into the house, and how you think it got out.

## AT THE MEETING; THE DOCTOR; EPILOGUE

**Vocabulary:** Draw a line from each word in column A to its synonym in column B. Then use the words in column A to fill in the blanks in the sentences below.

| A | B |
|---|---|
| 1. apparently | a. thin |
| 2. inexorable | b. unbelievingly |
| 3. sparse | c. tense |
| 4. nozzle | d. clearly |
| 5. incredulously | e. sent |
| 6. sentry | f. spout |
| 7. anxious | g. relentless |
| 8. dispatched | h. guard |

. . . . . . . . . . . . . . . . . . . . . . . . . . . . . . . . . . . . . . . . . . . . . . . . . . .

1. The fire department ________________ their trucks as soon as they received the alarm.
2. Afraid they would be robbed, the owners employed a(n) ________________ to watch the factory at night.
3. Jumping up and down, the children were ________________ excited about going to the circus.
4. Faced with the ________________ truth, the thief decided it was foolish to lie.
5. As the day of the performance came closer, the cast became ________________.
6. Point the ________________ of the hose toward the garden so the plants will receive the water they need.
7. The man responded ________________ when he was told he won the lottery.
8. Because the trees were ________________, the helicopter pilot was able to see the ground below.

Read to find out whether Mrs. Frisby will be safe from the plow.

**Questions:**

1. Why did Nicodemus ask Mrs. Frisby for all the details about the conversations she overheard at the Fitzgibbons'? Who did he suspect would be coming to destroy them?

## At the Meeting; The Doctor; Epilogue (cont.)

2. How did the rats plan to escape? Why did they plan to leave a rear guard of rats?
3. What happened to Brutus during the escape?
4. Why did Mrs. Frisby tell her children the whole story?
5. What was Martin's reaction to the story?

**Writing Activity:**

Mrs. Frisby and her family have moved to their summer home. What do you think life will be like there? Write a description of their home and tell about a typical day for the Frisby family.

## CLOZE ACTIVITY

The following passage has been taken from the chapter entitled "In the Cage." Read it through completely. Then go back and fill in each blank with one word that makes sense. Afterward you may compare your language with that of the author.

When my turn came, the door of my cage slid open just enough for Dr. Schultz to put his gloved hand through. I cowered to the back of the ____________,[1] which was just what he expected me ____________[2] do; one hand pressed me flat against ____________[3] wire wall; then his fingers gripped my ____________.[4] The other hand held my head just ____________[5] the ears, and I was powerless. I ____________[6] lifted from the cage and felt the ____________[7] collar clipped around my neck. I was ____________[8] inside with the door closed in less ____________[9] a minute. The collar was not tight, ____________[10] by no amount of tugging, twisting or ____________[11] was I ever able to get it ____________.[12]

I watched through the wire front of ____________[13] cage as the others were caught and ____________.[14] About six cages down from me, on ____________[15] same shelf, I saw them put a ____________[16] on Jenner; but once he was back ____________[17] his cage, I could see him no ____________.[18]

A little later in the morning they ____________[19] around again, this time pushing a table ____________[20] wheels. It was loaded with a bottle ____________[21] some clear liquid, a long rack of ____________[22] needles, and a plunger. Once more I ____________[23] lifted from the cage. This time George ____________[24] the holding while Dr. Schultz fastened one of ____________[25] needles to the plunger. I felt a ____________[26] pain in my hip; then it was ____________.[27] We all got used to that, for ____________[28] then on we got injections at least ____________[29] a week. What they were injecting and ____________,[30] I did not know. Yet for twenty of us those injections were to change our whole lives.

## POST-READING ACTIVITIES AND DISCUSSION QUESTIONS

1. *Mrs. Frisby and the Rats of NIMH* won the Newbery Medal in 1971, the year it was published. This is an award that is granted annually to the best young adult book as chosen by a committee of the American Library Association. Why do you think this book was chosen? Have you read any other Newbery winners? How do these books compare with Mrs. Frisby?
2. Return to the Character Chart that you began on page four of this study guide. Add additional information. Then compare your chart with those of your classmates.
3. Return to the Writing Activity on page nine of this study guide. Compare your predictions with the actual story.
4. Did this story change or reinforce your opinion about stealing? Is it ever all right to steal? Do you think the rats were actually stealing?
5. Use a Venn diagram to compare human society with the animal society created by the rats. Write about their similarities in the overlapping part of the circles.
6. Review the book and draw a map of the area that is the setting for the story. Include the Frisby house, the farmhouse, the rosebush, the owl's tree, and Thorn Valley.
7. Read at least one other book in which animals are treated as if they were people. Compare that book with *Mrs. Frisby and the Rats of NIMH*. Consider the following elements:
    - What parts of each story are fantasy? What parts are scientifically accurate?
    - How has the author made each story believable?
    - Are the plots well-constructed? Do they contain any inconsistencies?
    - Is each story logical?
    - Are the characters convincing?
    - What is the theme of each story?
8. Assume you are a newspaper reporter. Write an article about one of the following topics or a topic of your own choosing:
    - Intelligent rats being developed at NIMH
    - Moving of the Frisby home
    - The escape of the rats from NIMH
    - The escape of the rats from the rosebush
9. Read Rasco, the sequel to *Mrs. Frisby and the Rats of NIMH*, by Jane Leslie Conly, the daughter of Robert O'Brien. Learn how Mrs. Frisby and her family managed after they left the farm.

## POST-READING ACTIVITIES AND DISCUSSION QUESTIONS

10. **Cooperative Learning Activity:** The characters below are all animals and behave like animals in many ways. In addition, they have the ability to think, to feel, and to behave like humans. Work with a small group of your classmates to select from the list below those adjectives that describe each character. Use a dictionary to learn the meaning of any words you do not know. You may use a word more than once and you may add additional adjectives. Compare your responses with those of other groups.

*WORD BOX*

| | | |
|---|---|---|
| adventurous | daring | impetuous |
| aggressive | devoted | loyal |
| brilliant | frail | motherly |
| clever | generous | patient |
| courageous | gentle | responsible |
| cynical | helpful | stubborn |
| dangerous | hypochondriacal | wise |

| Mrs. Frisby | Timothy | Jeremy |
|---|---|---|
| | | |
| **Owl** | **Mr. Ages** | **Dragon** |
| | | |
| **Nicodemus** | **Jenner** | **Justin** |
| | | |

## SUGGESTIONS FOR FURTHER READING


* Adams, Richard. *Watership Down.* Scribner.

Alexander, Lloyd. *The Book of Three.* Square Fish.

________________. *The Black Cauldron.* Square Fish.

________________. *The Castle of Llyr.* Square Fish.

________________. *The High King.* Square Fish.

Arkin, Alan. *The Lemming Condition.* HarperCollins.

* Babbitt, Natalie. *Tuck Everlasting.* Holt McDougal.

Conly, Jane Leslie. *Rasco and the Rats of NIMH.* HarperCollins.

_________________. *R-T, Margaret, and the Rats of NIMH.* HarperCollins.

* Cooper, Susan. *The Dark is Rising.* Margaret K. Elderry Books.

* Grahame, Kenneth. *The Wind in the Willows.* Dover.

Lawson, Robert. *Rabbit Hill.* Puffin.

* L'Engle, Madeleine. *A Wrinkle in Time.* Square Fish.

* Lewis, C.S. *The Lion, the Witch and the Wardrobe.* HarperCollins.

Milne, A.A. *Winnie the Pooh.* Puffin.

* Norton, Mary. *The Borrowers.* HMH Books for Young Readers.

* Selden, George. *Cricket in Times Square.* Square Fish.

* Steig, William. *Abel's Island.* Square Fish.

* Tolkien. J.R.R. *The Hobbit.* Houghton Mifflin Harcourt.

* White, E.B. *Charlotte's Web.* HarperCollins.

* __________. *Stuart Little.* HarperCollins.

* __________. *Trumpet of the Swan.* HarperCollins.


**Other Books by Robert O'Brien**


*The Secret of NIMH.* Scholastic.

*The Silver Crown.* Aladdin.

*Z for Zachariah.* Simon Pulse.


* NOVEL-TIES Study Guides are available for these titles.

# ANSWER KEY

**The Sickness of Timothy Frisby; Mr. Ages; The Crow and the Cat**

Vocabulary: 1. g 2. a 3. h 4. b 5. e 6. d 7. c 8. f; 1. rancid 2. hypochondriac 3. relentlessly 4. delirious 5. authoritatively 6. temporary 7. abandoned 8. warily

Questions: 1. The Frisby family felt lucky to live in a slightly damaged cinder block on Mr. Fitzgibbon's farm because it was safe, snug, and close to a perpetual food source. 2. Mrs. Frisby went out hunting for food in winter because she hoped a change in their monotonous winter diet would help restore her ailing child's health. 3. On her food hunting walk, Mrs. Frisby was surprised to find a winter's supply of food carefully stored and then abandoned. 4. Mrs. Frisby sought Mr. Ages because she hoped he would be able to use his knowledge of medicinal herbs and plants to cure Timothy. 5. It was courageous of Mrs. Frisby to free Jeremy from the string which held him tied to the fence because crows may eat mice and this act also put her in danger of being seen by Dragon the cat.

**Mr. Fitzgibbon's Plow; Five Days; A Favor from Jeremy; The Owl**

Vocabulary: 1. f 2. g 3. h 4. b 5. d 6. e 7. a 8. c

Questions: 1. Mrs. Frisby knew that Moving Day was approaching because of the warm weather, the shrew's warning, and because the tractor would be fixed in five days. She was worried because Timothy was too sick to move. 2. Mrs. Frisby thought it was strange that the cat didn't chase her or bother the rats. It also seemed strange that the rats were marching in unison and were hauling a mysterious cable. Answers to the rest of the question will vary. 3. Jeremy repaid Mrs. Frisby's favor by taking her to the owl—the smartest bird—to solve her problem. 4. Mrs. Frisby meant that she feared owls because they eat mice.

**"Go to the Rats;" In the Rosebush; Brutus**

Vocabulary: 1. e 2. a 3. h 4. d 5. g 6. b 7. f 8. c; 1. cordial 2. linger 3. trespassers 4. deference 5. agitated 6. adjourned 7. affectionate 8. bewildered

Questions: 1. When the owl first met Mrs. Frisby, he was indifferent, offering no real solution. He changed when he learned that she was Jonathan Frisby's widow. 2. Both the owl and Mrs. Frisby needed to move and were reluctant to do so. 3. Mrs. Frisby was getting used to air travel. Since it was dark, she could not see the distance to the ground. 4. Timothy knew Moving Day was near because he smelled the frost melting. Mrs. Frisby was now expressing her worry and her child Timothy was consoling her. 5. Because the guards, Justin and Brutus, knew Mr. Ages and had great respect for Mr. Frisby, they allowed Mrs. Frisby to see Nicodemus. Mrs. Frisby wondered why they revered the memory of her late husband and consequently honored her by letting her see Nicodemus.

**In the Library; Isabella; A Powder for Dragon**

Vocabulary: 1. e 2. c 3. a 4. h 5. g 6. b 7. d 8. f; 1. glum 2. hostile 3. shallow 4. destination 5. swiftly 6. recessed 7. deserted 8. drowsy

Questions: 1. Mrs. Frisby thought it was unusual to observe an elevator, electric lights, and a library with books in the rats' hideaway. 2. Justin was referring to the rats' annual escapade of taking a few bulbs from Mr. Fitzgibbon's pine tree at Christmas time each year. 3. Mrs. Frisby learned that the rats had escaped from a place called NIMH; Nicodemus was the leader of the rat colony; they had a Plan for the future which involved leaving where they were living and storing grain; females sometimes didn't go to meetings; and Jenner didn't like the Plan and deserted. 4. The rats could help Mrs. Frisby by moving her house to the lee of the stone so that the plow would not destroy it. 5. Nicodemus was reluctant to allow Mrs. Frisby to plant the poison because it was a dangerous mission. In the past, similar missions resulted in Mrs. Ages' broken leg and Mr. Frisby's death.

**The Marketplace; In the Cage; The Maze**

Vocabulary: Across — 3. frenzy 4. confident 5. compiled 7. interior; Down — 1. maze 2. second 3. futile 4. converge 5. contrite 6. eager

Questions: 1. Nicodemus and his friend Jenner came to NIMH because they were out playing and getting food when they were captured by scientists. 2. The scientists captured the rats because they were using them in an experiment to see if a new form of DNA would make them more intelligent and if steroids would increase their life span. 3. Nicodemus described an experiment in which rats were put through a maze to find out how quickly they could learn. Another experiment concerned shape recognition, which led to actual teaching. 4. Although they were well-treated, the rats longed for freedom, an apparently hopeless dream. 5. Justin realized that the doctors had invested so much time and effort on the rats that they could not afford to have any harm come to them. 6. The doctors did not panic because they expected the escape attempt; it was part of their plan to test the results of the DNA and steroids. They learned that the injected rats were 300% ahead of the control group. A-9 discovered that there were experimental mice as well as experimental rats.

**A Lesson in Reading; The Air Ducts; The Boniface Estate**

Vocabulary: 1. e 2. b 3. h 4. c 5. g 6. a 7. d 8. f; 1. consternation 2. astute 3. comradeship 4. occasionally 5. partition 6. discontent 7. manipulated 8. reluctantly

Questions: 1. Unexpectedly, the rats became more intelligent than any rats had ever been, and their aging process seemed to stop almost completely as a result of the experimental treatment. 2. The scientists taught the rats to read by showing them a picture, showing them the letters, saying the letters, and then saying the word as they showed them the word and picture. 3. Nicodemus defined reading as the use of symbols to suggest a picture or an idea. 4. Taking advantage of the ability to read, Justin read the directions on the knob on his cage and figured out how to open it. Reading taught the rats how to escape. 5. When they were about to escape, Jenner realized that they were civilized rats and couldn't return to life in the sewer pipe; they didn't know where they wanted to live; and what would happen when Dr. Schultz announced that there was a group of civilized rats roaming loose. 6. It was revealed that Jonathan, Mrs. Frisby's late husband, had received the same experimental treatment as the rats, was just as smart as they, and had escaped with them. Only Jonathan and Mr. Ages, of the eight original mice, survived the passage. 7. To escape from NIMH, Justin and two other rats explored the air conditioning ducts, using a thread so they could find their way back. When they found the route, they all assembled, freed the mice, and got to the opening. Six of the mice were lost in the current caused by the motor, but Jonathan and Mr. Ages opened the screen and escaped. The rats escaped through the air-conditioning duct work which was similar to the mazes they had learned to negotiate during the experiments. 8. Although there was food for a year, the rats were most thrilled by the books at the Boniface Estate.

Special Activity: Message — To open cage turn lower handle around twice.

**The Main Hall, The Toy Tinker, Thorn Valley**

Vocabulary: 1. engrossed – engaged completely 2. skeptical – doubtful 3. confer – consult 4. cultivated – plowed 5. intentionally – purposely 6. pessimist – person who believes things will turn out badly

Questions: 1. The Plan was to live without stealing by using the seed they had stolen from Mr. Fitzgibbon's barn to start their farm. 2. The rats learned that they were the most hated creatures on earth; were valued as experimental animals; and were related to prairie dogs who, millions of years before, seemed to be making a civilization of their own. 3. The rats got tools and motors from the Toy Tinker which were perfect for them because they were nearly all miniature. 4. The rats became dissatisfied with life on the farm because it posed no challenge: life was too easy. Also, their new life style required more thievery. 5. Nicodemus met the old owl who was curious to know about the rats. He suggested Thorn Valley because the plower never came near it and was too rocky and steep for humans. 6. Jenner believed stealing electricity and food from humans was no worse than humans taking milk from cows. It just indicated that rats were smarter than people.

**Captured; Seven Dead Rats; Escape**

Vocabulary: 1. criticized 2. vertical 3. baffled 4. enormous 5. impasse 6. schedule 7. ventilation

Questions: 1. Jonathan never told Mrs. Frisby about NIMH because he didn't know how to explain why others would continue to grow older and he wouldn't. 2. Jenner left because he disagreed with the Plan, especially the part that called for destroying the machines. He and his friends were later electrocuted in the hardware store. 3. The rats decided to destroy their cave and the machines because they wanted to remove any temptation to return during the difficult times they might have in the beginning. 4. Mrs. Frisby put sleeping powder into Dragon's bowl so that he wouldn't disturb the rats as they moved the house. 5. Mrs. Frisby is caught and put into a birdcage. She perceives the colander with its holes as a curved ceiling with half moon lights. 6. Mrs. Frisby overhears that Federal agents are coming to exterminate the rats. 7. Mr. Fitzgibbon thinks the Federal agents want to destroy the rats because they spread rabies. Answers to the second part of the question will vary. 8. Justin does not want to arouse the Fitzgibbons' suspicions by opening a door that would ordinarily be impossible for mice to budge. This way it appears that a defective hinge fell open by itself.

**At the Meeting; The Doctor; Epilogue**

Vocabulary: 1. d 2. g 3. a 4. f 5. b 6. h 7. c 8. e; 1. dispatched 2. sentry 3. apparently 4. inexorable 5. anxious 6. nozzle 7. incredulously 8. sparse

Questions: 1. Nicodemus asked Mrs. Frisby what she overheard because he wanted to know who was coming after them, when they were coming, and why they were coming. He suspected the scientists from NIMH were coming to destroy them. 2. To escape from the rosebush, the rats planned to move everything to the main cave and then fill in the stairway and the elevator shaft. They would leave only the small storage room and tunnels leading to it. They would then fill the hole with garbage so it would look as if it housed only ordinary rats. All of the rats except for ten, who would form a rear guard, would then leave for Thorn Valley. If there were no rats in the hole, the men from NIMH would become suspicious and continue digging. 3. During the escape, Brutus was one of the rear guard who provided a diversion. He swallowed some of the gas and became unconscious shortly after making it into the woods. After the men from NIMH left, he was rescued by Mrs. Frisby and Mr. Ages. 4. Mrs. Frisby told her children the whole story because she believed they might have inherited some of their father's intelligence; thus, they might be very different from ordinary mice. 5. Martin was excited about the story and wanted to go to Thorn Valley. He hoped to find Jeremy in the fall and have the crow take him to Thorn Valley.